Kobe Bryant

Kobe Bryant

Michael Bradley

BENCHMARK BOOKS

MARSHALL CAVENDISH
NEW YORK

Benchmark Books
Marshall Cavendish
99 White Plains Road
Tarrytown, NY 10591-9001
www.marshallcavendish.com

Library of Congress Cataloging-in-Publication Data

Bradley, Michael, 1962-
Kobe Bryant / by Michael Bradley.
p. cm.—(Benchmark all-stars)
Includes bibliographical references and index.
Contents: Making his mark—Hoop roots—The big jump—The big
challenge—Onward and upward—A champion at last.
ISBN 0-7614-1629-3
1. Bryant, Kobe, 1978—Juvenile literature. 2. Basketball
players—United States—Biography—Juvenile literature. [1. Bryant,
Kobe, 1978- 2. Basketball players. 3. African Americans—Biography.] I.
Title. II. Series.

GV884.B794B73 2003
796.323'092—dc21

2003007085

Series design by Becky Terhune

Printed in Italy
1 3 5 6 4 2

Contents

Oh, my! Bryant heads to the hoop, with no one close enough to stop him.

CHAPTER ONE
Making His Mark

The loss had been an ugly one. The scoreboard said it all: Bulls 106, Lakers 104. These were not Michael Jordan's Chicago Bulls of the 1990s, filled with championship *potential*. This was 2002, and the Bulls were dead last in the National Basketball Association's (NBA) Central Division. Still, the last-place Bulls managed to outscore the Los Angeles Lakers. Then there was the *suspension*. Los Angeles center Shaquille O'Neal had been tossed out of the game and later suspended for three games for throwing a punch at a Chicago player. He had snapped. He then sat.

It was not the best time to be wearing the Lakers' colors. Even Kobe Bryant, the team's star guard, was upset. Bryant had missed all six of his field-goal attempts during the game's overtime period. He had also missed three important foul shots, including one with seven and a half seconds left in the game.

"Those . . . free shots," Bryant said after the game. "Man. Ugly. Ugly . . . I wish I could get it back, take it back, but I can't. So, I'm going to have to suck it up, take it on the chin, let them celebrate, throw down the confetti or whatever."

The two-time defending NBA championship Lakers then boarded a plane and flew back

Bryant is all smiles after another Lakers victory.

to Los Angeles where the Memphis Grizzlies would later join them. It was revenge time for the Lakers. Even though Shaquille O'Neal was unavailable thanks to the suspension, Bryant was still there. And he exploded.

Bryant drew the number thirty-four, O'Neal's uniform number, on his sneakers with a Magic Marker in tribute to his teammate. Then in just three quarters, Bryant scored a career-high 56 points in an easy 120–81 win over the Grizzlies. It was an amazing performance. He made 21 of 34 field-goal attempts and had 36 points at the half. Had the game been closer, Bryant might have surpassed Elgin Baylor's Lakers franchise record of 71 points. As it was, he was beyond impressive.

"That was one of the most incredible things you'll probably ever see," Los Angeles forward

Robert Horry said. "Words can't describe what that cat did tonight. He was unreal."

When it was all over, the interviewers wanted to know what message Bryant had for O'Neal. Bryant said, "I love you, man."

It was the perfect ending to a perfect performance. It was also yet another chapter in the life of one of the NBA's most exciting young players. Once the target of criticism for joining the league right out of high school, Kobe Bryant has become one of professional basket-

Kobe Bryant and Ron Artest, then of the Chicago Bulls, chase a loose ball in a game played early in 2002.

ball's brightest stars. He already has three *championship rings*. He has played in four NBA All-Star Games. He has won a *slam-dunk contest*. His high school retired his jersey.

Bryant's life is almost as impressive off the court. He is one of professional sports' most in-demand product *endorsers*. He can be seen in advertisements for Adidas, McDonald's, Spalding, and Upper Deck. He owns a $13.5 million mansion in southern California. He has appeared on numerous television programs and has even recorded a rap CD. Bryant is also part owner of an Italian professional team. (He spent the first eight years of his life in Italy.)

There are superstars, and then there is Kobe Bryant.

"He's one of the new generation of athletes who will help transform sports in the next decade or two," Adidas America president Steve Wynne said.

Bryant is much more than just a gifted athlete. He is a thoughtful, intelligent young

The Sixers' Todd MacCulloch is no match for a high-flying Kobe Bryant on his way to the hoop for a dunk.

man. He didn't skip college because he couldn't do the work. He had a 3.0 high school grade point average and scored nearly 1,100 on his SATs. Bryant became the youngest person ever to play in an NBA game because he knew it was time to make the move. It was time to test his skills at the highest level, against the very best. He was mature enough to handle the lifestyle and dedicated enough to the game to be prepared.

[**"He's one of the new generation of athletes who will help transform sports in the next decade or two."**
—Steve Wynne]

Sure he had some growing pains, but Bryant became a star well before his twenty-fifth birthday.

And he did it his way. The Charlotte Hornets drafted Bryant, but he didn't want to play for them. He asked his agent to work out a deal that would get him to the Los Angeles Lakers. And even though he started slowly, fans and longtime basketball experts knew he was something special. Before long, those few people skeptical of Bryant's talent bit back their negative words. Kobe Bryant had arrived. And his story was just beginning.

Here I come! While a senior at Lower Merion High School, Kobe shows what's in store for opponents who get in his way.

CHAPTER TWO

Hoop Roots

Just about everyone knew Kobe Bryant was going to be tall. His father, former NBA player Joe Bryant, measures 6'9". His grandfather stood 6'5". The *genes* were there. From the time Kobe was three years old, Kobe wanted to play in the NBA. He would put on a kid-size replica of his father's San Diego Clippers uniform and shoot his Nerf basketball into a toy net.

"He'd tell me, even then, 'Mom, I'm going to play in the NBA,'" Pam Bryant said.

His father, Joe Bryant, had been a standout player at Philadelphia's John Bartram High School. He went on to score 1,118 career points at La Salle University, also in Philadelphia. Though never an All-Star, Joe Bryant spent eight years in the NBA, with Philadelphia, Houston, and San Diego, averaging 8.7 points per game (ppg) for his career.

Basketball was the Bryant family business, and Kobe wanted to be a part of it. When Kobe was nine and living in Italy with his family, he would tell his friends that he was going to be an NBA star. When they laughed at him, he would write his name on a piece of paper and give it to them. "You might want to hold on to this," he would say. Those

Kobe Bryant celebrates the Lakers' 2000 NBA championship by planting a big kiss on his father, Joe Bryant.

who did have the autograph of an All-Star—and of somebody who knew he would succeed.

Kobe Bryant was born on August 23, 1978, in Philadelphia, just before his father's fourth and final season with the 76ers. He was the third of three children and the only boy in the bunch, behind sisters Sharia and Shaya. The Bryants bounced from San Diego (three years) to Houston (one) before embarking on a true basketball adventure—to Italy. Joe Bryant signed a contract to play there, and the family spent eight seasons abroad. They lived in small towns, learned the language and the culture, and enjoyed their life together.

"We're all about family," Joe Bryant said. "We're kind of old-fashioned that way. We all look after each other, with genuine care."

That all-for-one attitude developed in Italy, where life seemed to revolve around family. Kobe Bryant knew that no matter what happened at school or on the court, he would be loved by his family.

> "We're all about family. We're kind of
> old-fashioned that way. We all look
> after each other, with genuine care."
> —Joe Bryant

"The backbone is the family," he said. "Once you have that, then everything else is cool. Whether you score 50 points or 0, your family is gonna be there. The Italians have that same thing. They're very warm-hearted people. We were very comfortable there. We fell right in it."

Those strong family ties would help him later when he was making his decision to enter the NBA draft. While everybody else offered advice and wondered what Kobe was going to do, he relied on his family—and especially his father—for support. The two grew to be best friends and were practically *inseparable* off the court. While other boys spent their free time with classmates, Kobe spent time with his parents. They watched movies together and had long conversations. And never once did Kobe seem shy about hugging or kissing either of his parents in public.

"I think it's because we all grew up together in Italy," he said. "We didn't have anybody to depend on but our family. We had to stick together."

Kobe was fourteen when the Bryants returned to Philadelphia. And he knew no one. On his first day of

Basketball in Italy

The NBA may have the world's best basketball, but plenty of good action can be found in Europe, especially in Italy.

For many years, the best players in the Italian League were Americans who were not good enough to play in the NBA or older players looking to prolong their professional careers. Not anymore. Although there are still a good number of Americans who play in the league, Italians are getting better every year.

There are two leagues in Italy, "Serie A," the top conference, and "Lega 2." Each year, the winner of Lega 2 moves up to Serie A. The Italian regular season lasts only about thirty games, less than half of the NBA's eighty-two games. And the winner of the playoffs then competes in the European Championships. In the late 1990s, an NBA team would play some exhibition games against better teams from Europe. Despite the improvement of basketball across the Atlantic, none of the better teams from Europe would be able to compete on the same level as NBA clubs, particularly over the course of a full season.

Italian fans are extremely passionate about their teams, and visiting clubs are often harassed and heckled far more than NBA opponents are. Some of the better Italian League teams are Kinder Bologna, Benetton Treviso, and Skipper Bologna.

Family played a big role in Kobe's growth and development. Here, he poses with his mother and one of his sisters.

middle school, Kobe was eating his lunch when a classmate approached him and said, "I hear you're a pretty good basketball player." Kobe said he was, and the other boy challenged him to a game. It wasn't much of a contest.

"I played him after school, and I shut him out," Kobe said. "And I got my respect right there. That's what I was looking for all my years in Italy."

It wasn't always that easy on the court. Although Kobe had been *dominant* in Italy, he struggled against competition in America. During the summers after his sixth and seventh grades, he returned to Philadelphia and played in a local league. The players were more *aggressive* and physical than anyone he had faced in Italy. Kobe struggled. He did not score for two summers. Not one point.

"We always felt he would be a player," said Tony Sammartino, director of the Philadelphia league. "But he was scared to death playing with the city kids."

When the Bryants went back to Italy after the second summer, Kobe started playing basketball whenever he could. He worked on every part of his game, and when he returned to the same summer league in the United States after his eighth-grade year, he was named its most valuable player.

From there Kobe was unstoppable. He became the star of the Lower Merion High School team as a sophomore, and by the time he was a junior, the nation was learning about him.

"Kobe Bryant reminds me a great deal of Grant Hill," respected talent evaluator Bob Gibbons said in April 1995. "He is the most skilled player in the junior class that I've seen, and I've been coast-to-coast. At 6'6", Bryant has point-guard skills. He can shoot the ball, and he's a wonderful passer and excellent defensive player. It's the old cliche: He's the total package."

Kobe averaged 31.1 points, 10.4 *rebounds*, 5.2 *assists*, 3.8 blocks, and 2.3 steals a game as a junior. Lower Merion High School won its league title and advanced to the state play-offs, where Kobe continued to earn praise and fans.

"I don't know of any player in the area that is better," said Sonny Hill, a longtime Philadelphia basketball expert. "He is among the more unique talents we've had in a long, long time."

Hill was right. Soon all of America would know just how right.

Kobe announces to the world that he will enter the NBA draft following his high school graduation.

CHAPTER THREE
The Big Jump

It was D-day. Decision day. Kobe Bryant stood behind a lectern, sunglasses resting atop his shiny, clean-shaven head, ready to make his announcement. The stands of Lower Merion High School's gymnasium were packed with students. Reporters, television cameras, and dozens of other interested people waited for the news. The Bryant family stood behind him, offering support.

It was all happening. After months of speculation, Kobe Bryant was going to tell the world what he wanted to do. Would it be college, or would it be the NBA?

The subject had dominated the Philadelphia basketball scene for months. Even though Joe Bryant was an assistant coach at La Salle University, his alma mater, Kobe had not guaranteed that he would play ball there. He wouldn't commit to any other college, either. No matter how hard people pressed, Kobe wouldn't tell. His friends didn't know. His high school coach didn't know. And, in some ways, Kobe didn't know, either.

"With Kobe, it's a roller-coaster ride," Joe Bryant said. "He sees college games, he sees the excitement, and he gets excited and wants to be a part of that. Then he sees an NBA game. He watches [guard] Penny Hardaway, and he says, 'I can play with those guys.' He

Kobe squeezes through the opposition for two more points during his spectacular career at Lower Merion High School.

has to wait until all the emotion is gone and decide what is the best choice for him."

In the 1995-1996 season, the choice for Kobe was Lower Merion High School. After leading his team, the Aces, to the state tournament as a junior, Kobe was determined to win a state championship. His performance certainly showed how much he wanted it. He averaged 30.8 ppg and ended his time in high school with 2,883 points, the most ever scored by a southeastern Pennsylvania high schooler. Kobe led Lower Merion to a 31 and 3 record. In the state title game, he scored 17 points, had 9 rebounds, and 3 assists, for a Lower Merion win (48–43) over Erie Cathedral Prep and the championship. He had achieved his goal.

After the game he hugged

his father while the sellout crowd cheered. Reporters swarmed around him and asked the question everybody wanted an answer to: NBA or college? Bryant wasn't telling.

"It's going to take a lot of time and thinking about whether I'm ready to make that jump," he said.

While Bryant tried to consider his options, scouts, analysts, and other "experts" debated whether he was ready for the NBA. Some said he had the skills to play there. Others wondered whether his slim body could handle the league's tough play. The other players who had moved on to the professional league from high school—including Moses Malone, Darryl Dawkins, Bill Willoughby, and Kevin Garnett—had been big men. No guard had ever tried it. Many at the college level criticized Kobe. They said he should play a couple of years at a college so he could mature. Everybody, it seemed, had an opinion.

"Kevin Garnet's ability as a [6'11"] player was so overwhelming it came through immediately," one scout said. "He's a very special player. You watch Kobe Bryant, and you don't see that. His game doesn't say, 'I'm a very special talent.'"

After all the arguing, Bryant was finally ready to make his announcement. The crowd grew quiet. Kobe smiled broadly.

⭐ **From High School to the NBA**

Kobe Bryant was neither the first nor the last player ever to make the jump from high school to the NBA. He just may be the most successful.

It began in 1974 when 6'11" Moses Malone decided to move from Petersburg, Virginia, to the old American Basketball Association (ABA), which was an NBA competitor for nine seasons (1967 to 1976). Malone played for the Utah Stars and the Spirits of St. Louis before joining the NBA when the ABA folded. Malone was a three-time Most Valuable Player and helped the Philadelphia 76ers to the 1983 NBA championship. Before Kobe Bryant, Malone was the most successful player to bypass college for the NBA. Two others, Bill Willoughby and Darryl Dawkins, enjoyed moderate success.

There are several current NBA players who didn't spend a day in college. Among the more successful are Minnesota's Kevin Garnett, Orlando's Tracy McGrady, Indiana's Jermaine O'Neal, Cleveland's Darius Miles, and Seattle's Rashard Lewis. But not every player who has made the move has met with the same success.

Kobe Bryant may have some company in the NBA, but it isn't easy to move from the high school level right to the big time.

Even Kobe found it difficult to imagine what lay ahead of him when he made the jump to the NBA.

"Hi, I'm Kobe Bryant," he said. "And I've decided to take my talent to . . ." He scratched his chin. He pretended that he didn't know. He knew. "Well, I have decided to skip college and take my talent to the NBA."

The students cheered. His parents smiled proudly. Then came the questions. Bryant had all the answers.

"It's a great challenge," he said. "I'm a person who loves competitiveness, and I want to go out there and do the best I can with the best competition."

Bryant had made his decision, but the real work was only beginning. It seemed every NBA team wanted to meet him and watch him play. Many were impressed.

"Kobe was, by far, the most skilled player we've ever worked out," Los Angeles Lakers general manager Jerry West said.

On draft day the Charlotte Hornets chose Kobe Bryant with the thirteenth pick of the first round. It was an honor to be drafted that high, especially since Bryant was only seventeen years old. But Kobe didn't want to play for the Hornets. He wanted to be a Laker. So, Charlotte traded him to Los Angeles. It was almost too perfect.

"Most players, when they're drafted, rarely have the opportunity to have their dreams fulfilled," said Bryant's agent, Arn Tellem. "But we were in a position to do it, so we went for it, and we achieved it."

Just like that, it was good-bye Philadelphia and hello Los Angeles. Joe and Pam Bryant went West with their son. So did his sister Shaya, who would go to Pepperdine University in Malibu. Sharia stayed back home to play volleyball for Temple University. Kobe Bryant signed a three-year, $3.5 million contract with the Lakers. He bought a six-bedroom house in the sunny Pacific Palisades. He bought two cars: a BMW and a Land Cruiser. The dream was a reality. Soon, it would be time to show what he could do.

From the earliest moments of his professional career, it was clear that Bryant had the talent and poise to be a star.

CHAPTER FOUR

The Challenge

Kobe Bryant was a Laker. He was ready to take the NBA by storm. But he would have to wait. Less than two months before the start of the 1996-1997 season—Bryant's first— he broke his left wrist while playing a pickup basketball game in Venice Beach, California. After impressing everybody during the Los Angeles Summer Pro League (he averaged 24 ppg), Bryant was eager to play for real.

It took more than four weeks for his wrist to heal, but he was back on the court in time to play in some preseason games. Then came more trouble.

During one game Bryant fell and bruised his hip. That earned him a trip to the injured list and kept him out of the Lakers' first two regular-season games.

"Kobe [has] to learn a little patience," teammate Shaquille O'Neal said after the second injury.

He would have to learn more than a little patience. Instead of making an instant impact with the Lakers, Bryant was a substitute player. The Lakers already had a good shooting guard—Bryant's position—in Eddie Jones. Instead of becoming an instant star in Los Angeles, Bryant took some time to learn the NBA game. He wasn't thrilled with the idea,

The Lakers Tradition

Although the Boston Celtics' sixteen NBA championships are the most by any franchise, the Lakers, with fourteen wins, are the second-most successful team in the league's history.

The Lakers became a team in 1948 in Minneapolis. They took the Lakers nickname because of the many lakes throughout the state of Minnesota. Led by 6'11" center George Mikan, the Lakers won five NBA titles from 1949 to 1955, establishing themselves as the league's first dynasty.

The Lakers moved to Los Angeles in 1960 but didn't win the championship again until 1972. That year the great Wilt Chamberlain and Jerry West helped the team to a record sixty-nine regular-season wins, including thirty-three in a row.

In the 1980s, Los Angeles won five championships with the dynamic duo of Kareem Abdul-Jabbar and Magic Johnson. Add in the three straight championships won by Kobe Bryant and Shaquille O'Neal during the first years of the twenty-first century, and you can see why the Lakers are one of the most storied franchises in NBA history.

but he decided to do his best, no matter what his role was with the team.

> "Kobe [has] to learn a little patience."
> —Shaquille O'Neal

"I think about challenges all the time, and this is the ultimate challenge," he said. "You get a chance to learn from the best. If they're killing you, if they're beating you up, they're teaching you at the same time. Only positives can come out of it. I'm not nervous, and I'm not scared."

Bryant's first year with the Lakers was filled with both highlights and tough times. An undeniable high point was his win in the slam-dunk contest at the 1997 NBA All-Star Game. His winning jam raised his score to 49 out of 50. Bryant raced down the middle of the lane, put the ball under his right leg with his left hand, grabbed it with his right hand, and stuffed it through.

Earlier, although he had scored 31 points in the Western Conference rookie all-star game, his team lost 96 to 91. Despite his great performances in the slam-dunk contest and rookie game, Bryant was still a reserve for the Lakers. He averaged just 7.6 ppg and played only 15.5 minutes per night. After the season, Bryant was voted to the NBA's All-Rookie Second Team. He didn't complain, but he was clearly hoping for more. He also had some trouble with veteran players, who thought he was too confident in his abilities. Even Shaquille O'Neal, his teammate, called him "Showboat."

Bryant didn't worry. He kept on working hard. "I just try to do my job," he said.

No one with the Lakers was upset with his performance. Bryant did a fine job, particularly considering he was just eighteen years old and that he had missed a large chunk of training camp with the wrist injury. Though some around the league thought he wasn't respectful enough toward his elders, most considered his rookie year a success, including his coach.

"I said from the outset I was going to treat him like any other player because he's

> **"I think about challenges all the time, and this is the ultimate challenge. You get a chance to learn from the best. . . . Only positives can come out of it. I'm not nervous, and I'm not scared."**
>
> **—Kobe Bryant**

Kobe Bryant holds aloft the trophy he won as the 1997 NBA Slam Dunk champion at the annual All-Star Weekend.

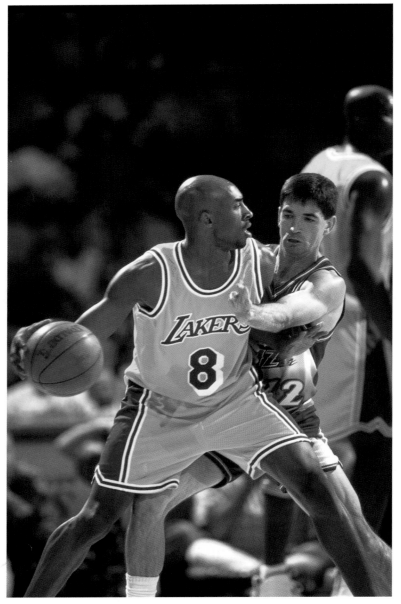

Old school versus new school: Veteran Utah Jazz guard John Stockton checks Kobe Bryant during a 1998 playoff game.

jumping into a man's world, and he has to deal with it," said Del Harris, the Lakers' coach at the time. "I wanted him to have to work for what he got. He hasn't gotten a lot yet, but he has worked. He's totally dedicated, and he has wonderful potential. He [has] actually shown us he's at least as good, if not better, than we thought."

Bryant's potential became more of a reality during his second season. His scoring jumped. He played more minutes. And fewer people cared that he had come right to the NBA from high school. He was now a Laker, not an eighteen-year-old rookie. He was still learning the game, but he was more comfortable as a professional.

"The transition was a lot smoother this year," Bryant said. "Coach Harris has always treated me as just another basketball player. He's hard on me, but that's because he wants me to be a great player. Every mistake I make, he lets me know—even the very tiny ones. But those are the things that pay off and win championships or lose championships."

Bryant averaged 15.4 ppg during the 1997-1998 campaign and saw his playing time climb to 26 minutes per game. He had some great moments, like when he scored 27 points in just 16 minutes against the Houston Rockets. That impressed Rockets' All-Star Guard Clyde Drexler.

"Kobe is a phenomenal player," Drexler said. "I really love his game. He reminds me of a guy named Michael Jordan."

Just two days later, Bryant scored 30 points against Dallas.

"Give Kobe a couple more years, and he might be 'The Man' of the whole league," Dallas guard Dennis Scott said.

Michael Jordan himself jumped aboard the Kobe Bryant train a couple of days later. Bryant scored 33 points against the Chicago Bulls, including a tremendous dunk.

"I turned to [Chicago teammate] Scottie Pippen and asked, 'Did we jump like that when we were nineteen?'" Jordan said. "[Bryant] has a lot of skills."

The praise was great, but all was not perfect. In the Lakers' final playoff game, against the Utah Jazz, Bryant missed four shots in overtime, and Los Angeles lost the series to Utah. The critics loved that. They said Bryant was impatient. They said he wanted to take all the shots. Bryant took the criticism with the praise and continued his growth.

"The first couple of years, it probably would have been more fun if I went to a [losing] team like the Sixers or Clippers or something, because I would have been putting up 30 shots a night, and it would have been fun," Bryant said. "But it might have taken six, seven years to learn what I have [learned] in a couple of seasons. Everybody here—[former Lakers] Magic [Johnson], Jerry West—they share their knowledge with you. So, it was definitely worth it."

> **"He reminds me of a guy named Michael Jordan."**
> **—Clyde Drexler**

Having broken cleanly from the pack, Kobe Bryant soars in for a two-handed jam against the Portland Trailblazers.

CHAPTER FIVE

Onward and Upward

Once Shaquille O'Neal stopped calling Bryant "Showboat," he came up with a new way to describe his young teammate.

"I'm the big brother," O'Neal said. "He's the little brother."

That's how it was in Los Angeles. O'Neal was "The Man," the giant center with the big contract and veteran status. Bryant was still finding his way, looking for more minutes on the court. He was still learning. Even though his second year had been a big improvement on his rookie season, Bryant had struggled in the 1998 playoffs, first with the flu, against Seattle, and later with his poor shooting in the Lakers' final game, against Utah.

He wanted to move on, but he couldn't do it right away. The start of the 1998-1999 season was delayed three months by a dispute between the NBA and its players. The players wanted bigger salaries and more freedom to move from team to team. League owners didn't want to give in. They fought and argued. Nobody played.

By late January the trouble was over, and the season began. But not before the Lakers and Bryant took care of some business. On January 29, 1999, Bryant signed a six-year-contract extension worth nearly $71 million. It was a big step for him and proof that the team wanted him to be a Laker for a long time.

Here's a sight that can bring fear to other NBA teams: the Lakers' Dynamic Duo, Shaquille O'Neal and Kobe Bryant.

"We're very pleased to get this contract done," Lakers general manager Jerry West said. "As I've said since we traded for Bryant back in 1996, we think he's one of the most talented young players in the NBA. He's going to continue to improve and make us a better team."

About a month into the season, Bryant got some good news. Los Angeles traded Eddie Jones to Charlotte, clearing the way for Bryant to become a full-time starter. Even though Bryant was just twenty years old and in his third year with the NBA, he was on his way. He responded by having his best year as a professional. Bryant averaged 19.9 ppg, 5.3 rebounds per game (rpg) and 3.8 assists per game (apg)—all career highs. He shot 46.5 percent from the field, his best percentage ever.

Bryant was on a roll, but the Lakers were not. They beat the Houston Rockets in the first round of the playoffs but were swept by the San Antonio Spurs in the Western Conference semifinals. Even though Bryant was a rising star and O'Neal was the backbone of the team, the Lakers needed a change. They needed a coach who could fit the pieces together.

That coach was Phil Jackson. He had led Michael Jordan and the Chicago Bulls to six world championships. He came to Los Angeles to help the Lakers win again. In the 1980s Los Angeles had won five crowns. It was time for more. First, Jackson would have to get Bryant and O'Neal together. Many believed the two players were jealous of each other and cared more about their own point totals than the team's success. Jackson wanted them to play team basketball, to worry about winning, not personal glory. At first there were some problems, but Bryant and O'Neal worked hard to blend their talents together.

The 1999-2000 season began with big hopes for the Lakers. Jackson was a proven winner, and he would teach O'Neal and Bryant how to succeed. The two players had already decided they should try to be better teammates. O'Neal took a step in that direction in August, when he went to Bryant's twenty-first birthday party. "Me and Bryant are cool," O'Neal said. "We got to know each other, and we found that there's room in this offense for us both to do our thing."

Bryant agreed. Since both he and O'Neal were great scorers, there would be times when each would have to wait his turn while the other shot the ball. If they did that, then the wins would come.

"We're both attackers," Bryant said during the 1999-2000 season. "We both want to get 40 points. I had to figure out how to attack in a different way. I've got it pretty much figured out now—not completely, but almost."

Kobe Bryant's game isn't all offense. Here, he tries to stop Houston's Scottie Pippen from scoring in the lane.

Both Bryant and O'Neal appeared to have it pretty well under control. O'Neal had perhaps his best season as a pro, averaging 29.7 ppg and 13.6 rpg. He was named the most valuable player (MVP). Bryant enjoyed his finest year too. He scored 22.5 ppg and grabbed 6.3 rpg, moving closer to becoming one of the league's biggest stars. But Bryant wasn't all about scoring.

In February he helped shut down the Philadelphia 76ers' Allen Iverson in the fourth quarter of a big, 87–84 Lakers win. Bryant forced Iverson to shoot 0 for 9 during the fourth quarter and blocked Iverson's final shot. On March 9, the Golden State Warriors' Larry Hughes scored 41 points—many of them against

Meeting of the minds: Kobe Bryant and Shaquille O'Neal celebrate a 2002 playoff win over Portland.

Bryant—in another Lakers win. Thirteen days later the teams met again, and Bryant was determined to prove himself to Hughes. He did that, playing great defense and helping Los Angeles to a lopsided win.

The Lakers had plenty of nights like that. They rolled to a 67 and 15 record, by far the best in the league—and just five wins less than the best in NBA history. But Los Angeles had been great in the regular season before. It was time to get it done in the playoffs. It was time for Big Brother and Little Brother to get serious.

Kobe Bryant prepares to rise in the lane for a shot during the 2000 NBA finals as Indiana guard Reggie Miller looks to stop him.

CHAPTER SIX
A Champion at Last

*J*ust a few days before the fourth game of the 2000 NBA Finals, things were not looking good for the Lakers. Bryant had to be helped off the Lakers' home court, the Forum, with a sprained ankle. After shooting a jump shot, he had landed on the foot of Indiana Pacers guard Jalen Rose. It was a painful injury—and it came at the worst time.

The Lakers had made it to the finals. Their goal was within reach.

And even though Los Angeles was able to beat the Pacers without Bryant and take a 2 and 0 lead, the young guard was still upset. He would have to miss the third game of the series, in Indiana. This wasn't how it was supposed to be. But injuries don't follow a schedule. They come when they come. And Bryant was hurt.

"It was just pain; it was just flat-out pain," Bryant said after the game.

The Lakers dropped a 100–91 decision to the Pacers in Game 3. Their series lead was now just 2 to 1. It was time for someone to step up for Los Angeles and make it happen.

That someone was Kobe Bryant.

Despite playing with an ankle he later described as "throbbing," Bryant was huge in the

Kobe Bryant grimaces in pain after injuring his ankle during a collision with Indiana's Jalen Rose during the 2000 NBA Finals.

fourth game. He scored 28 points and hit three key shots in over-time—after Shaquille O'Neal had fouled out—to lead the Lakers to a 120–118 win. It gave Los Angeles a commanding 3 to 1 series lead and established Bryant as a true star. He had delivered in the clutch. That's when the great ones do it.

"This is the game you dream about when you're growing up," he said. "You lose yourself in the moment. You're consumed by the game."

It was an amazing performance, especially since Bryant was just twenty-one years old. Here he was on basketball's brightest stage, lifting the Lakers to the brink of a world championship.

"Kobe took over," O'Neal said. "He's just a fabulous player."

Indeed he was. Even though the Pacers won the fifth game, Bryant scored 26 points in the sixth game to help the Lakers clinch the crown. O'Neal had 41 points and grabbed the finals' MVP award, but it was clear that Little Brother had grown up.

"That was big-time tonight," Lakers forward Glen Rice said about Bryant's Game 4 explosion. "That had to be the biggest performance since

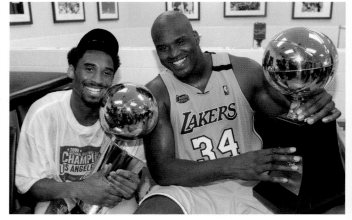

Kobe Bryant holds the NBA championship trophy while Shaquille O'Neal displays his finals MVP award, after the Lakers beat Indiana in 2000.

Kobe Bryant listens intently while Lakers coach Phil Jackson makes a point during practice.

I've been watching and playing with him, of his career. He stepped up like a veteran. That just goes to show how much he's matured."

Bryant had arrived. He had a championship ring. He had the respect of his peers. All the television commercials and fancy basketball shoes were nice, but none of it compared to winning.

As the 2000-2001 season dawned, the challenge was to repeat the previous year's success. Coach Phil Jackson had won three straight titles on two separate streaks while with the Chicago Bulls. That was a total of six titles! He wouldn't be satisfied with just one championship. He wanted more. So did Bryant. When he was a rookie, he said he wanted to win ten championships. It was time to work on number two.

The Lakers won the Pacific Division with a 56–26 record, and Bryant averaged a career high of 28.5 ppg and added 5.9 rpg. It wasn't easy to do. There were times during the year when Bryant and O'Neal feuded; times when the team didn't get along very well. By playoff time, though, everything was fine. Everybody was getting along, and the Lakers were ready to roll.

"I love these guys," Bryant said. "I don't think I've done anything different or made any changes in the way I am. But if the guys feel more comfortable around me than they once did, that's great."

> **"This is the game you dream about when you're growing up. You lose yourself in the moment. You're consumed by the game."**
>
> **—Kobe Bryant**

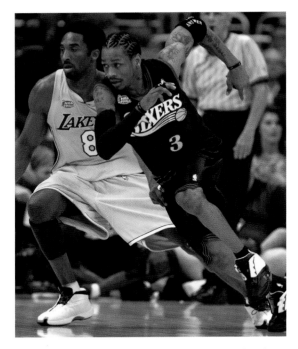

Philadelphia guard Allen Iverson looks for an opening during the 2001 NBA Finals, but Bryant is right there with him.

The Lakers rampaged their way through the Western Conference, sweeping Portland, Sacramento, and San Antonio. All that stood between them and a repeat title were the scrappy Philadelphia 76ers and star guard Allen Iverson.

Philly took the first game, surprising the Lakers in overtime. It would be the only bump in the playoff road for Los Angeles. Although the Sixers fought valiantly, they were no match for the dynamic duo of O'Neal and Bryant. Bryant averaged 24.6 points, 7 rebounds, and 5.8 assists per game. He scored 31 points in Game 2 and 32 in Game 3. When it was all over, the Lakers returned to Los Angeles and paraded their trophy through the streets. It was a fitting celebration for conquering heroes. And Bryant loved it.

"We told y'all last year we were going to do it again," he shouted to the crowds. "We did it again! We're going to get another one next year. Back to back to back!"

In 2002, just one year later, Kobe Bryant was back on the podium, celebrating another NBA title. The Lakers had beaten the New Jersey Nets in the finals, four games to none. Although Shaquille O'Neal was the series MVP, Bryant played a big role, as usual. In Game 3, he scored 36 points, including two big jump shots in the final minutes of a 106–103 Los

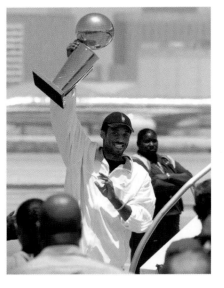

Bryant shows off the Lakers' 2001 NBA championship trophy after arriving home from clinching the title in Philadelphia.

Angeles win. He had 25 points in the deciding fourth game, 9 of which came in the fourth quarter of a 113–107 win.

Bryant was still two months shy of his twenty-fourth birthday, and he had three NBA championships to his credit already. Who knew what lay ahead. Then again, as Bryant spoke to the crowd at the Lakers' parade following the 2002 title win, it seemed like he knew.

"I told you all last year we're going back to back to back," he said to huge cheers. "I'll see you all next year."

It's hard not to believe him. After everything Kobe Bryant has accomplished in just twenty-four years, anything seems possible.

Kobe Bryant slams home two points against New Jersey during the 2002 NBA Finals.

stats

Stats

Kobe Bryant

Team: Los Angeles Lakers
Position: Guard
Born: August 23, 1978
Height: 6'6"
Weight: 220 lbs. (100 kg)
High School: Lower Merion, Pennsylvania

Career Averages

Year	Games	Games Started	Minutes Per Game	Field Goal%	3 point %	Free Throw %	Offense	Rebounds Per Game Defense	Rebounds Per Game	Assists Per Game
1996-97	71	6	15.5	.417	.375	.819	.70	1.20	1.90	1.3
1997-98	79	1	26.0	.428	.341	.794	1.00	2.10	3.10	2.5
1998-99	50	50	37.9	.465	.267	.839	1.10	4.20	5.30	3.8
1999-00	66	62	38.2	.468	.319	.821	1.60	4.70	6.30	4.9
2000-01	68	68	40.9	.464	.305	.853	1.50	4.30	5.90	5.0
2001-02	80	80	38.3	.469	.250	.829	1.40	4.10	5.50	5.5
2002-03	76	76	41.5	.451	.340	.837	1.30	5.60	6.90	5.9
Career	490	343	33.8	.456	.332	.829	1.20	3.60	4.90	4.1
Playoff	85	65	35.9	.441	.333	.778	1.20	3.60	4.80	4.1
All-Star	5	5	29.2	.473	.389	.800	1.80	2.30	4.60	4.4

Figures compiled from NBA.com. Statistics for 2003 are as of April 6, 2003.

GLOSSARY

aggressive—Bold; an aggressive player is willing to do whatever it takes to win.

assists—Passes which result directly in baskets scored by teammates.

championship rings—Fancy rings that are given to players on winning teams.

dominant—Commanding, or ruling others.

endorser—A person who helps improve the image and sales of a product by lending his or her name and image to it.

genes—Basic units of human development which influence the development of certain physical and mental traits. These are passed down from parents to children.

inseparable—Unable to be pulled apart.

potential—How well a person can do based on a variety of physical, emotional, and psychological factors, as well as prior performances.

rebounds—Balls that fail to go through the hoop and bounce off the rim or backboard, to be picked up by teammates or opponents.

slam-dunk contest—A competition, first held in 1976 in the American Basketball Association, in which players try to jam the ball in creative and athletic ways.

suspension—Temporary removal from play because of actions which are either illegal or damaging to the team.

FIND OUT MORE

Books

Christopher, Matt. *On the Court with Kobe Bryant*. New York: Little Brown & Co., 2001.

Coffey, Wayne R. *The Kobe Bryant Story*. New York: Scholastic Paperbacks, 1999.

Layden, Joseph. *Kobe: The Story of the NBA's Rising Star*. New York: Harper Mass Market Paperbacks, 1998.

Web Sites

NBA Official Site
Kobe Bryant
http://www.nba.com/playerfile/kobe_bryant?nav=page

CNN-Sports Illustrated
Kobe Bryant
http://sportsillustrated.cnn.com/basketball/nba/players/3118

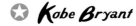

INDEX

Page numbers in **boldface** are illustrations.

PHOTO CREDITS

Photo research by Regina Flanagan.
Cover: John McDonough/Sports Illustrated
John McDonough/Sports Illustrated: 2–3, 6, 24, 28, 32, 34;
Reuters NewMedia/Corbis: 8, 14, 39, 40 (top and bottom);
AP/Wide World Photos: 9, 12, 18, 35, 41; Robert Beck/Sports
Illustrated: 10; Walter Ioos/Sports Illustrated: 16; Al
Tielemans/Sports Illustrated: 20; Neal Preston/Corbis: 22; David
Liam Kyle/Sports Illustrated: 27; John McDonough/SI/Icon
Sports Media: 30; Gerald Raube/Icon Sports Media: 36;
AFP/Corbis: 38 (top and bottom); Icon Sports Media: 42.